Movin'

edited by Dave Johnson
in association with
The New York Public Library
and Poets House

pictures by Chris Raschka

Orchard Books • New York
An Imprint of Scholastic Inc.

Thanks to The New York Public Library
and Poets House for asking.
Thanks to Orchard Books for
believing.—D.J.

Text copyright © 2000 by The New York Public Library, Astor, Lenox, and
Tilden Foundations
Illustrations copyright © 2000 by Chris Raschka

Library of Congress Cataloging-in-Publication Data
Movin': teen poets take voice / edited by Dave Johnson.
p.   cm.
"From works in the New York Public Library TeenLink and
Poetry-in-the-Branches projects."
ISBN 0-531-30258-X (trade : alk. paper)—ISBN 0-531-07171-5 (pbk. : alk. paper)
1. Teenagers' writings, American. 2. Young adult poetry, American. 3. Teenagers—
Poetry. 4. American poetry. 5. American poetry—20th century. I. Johnson, Dave.
II. New York Public Library. III. Poetry-in-the-Branches
(Project : New York Public Library)
PS549.N5 M68 1999
811'.540809283'09747—dc21   99-49455

10 9 8 7 6 5 4 3 2
Printed in the U.S.A.   13

Book design by Vicki Fischman
The text of this book is set in 12 point Usherwood.
The illustrations are pen and ink and watercolor.

Contents

Acknowledgments

THIS BOOK would never have become a reality without many dedicated and poetry-loving people. Chief among these are the knowledgeable and enthusiastic staff of Poets House: Lee Briccetti, executive director, who initiated the Poetry-in-the-Branches project; Jane Preston, managing director; and Catherine Coy, program director. They have brought their combined passion for poetry to the goal of making it a vital part of everyone's lives—young adults and librarians alike. None of this could have been possible without Sheila Murphy, who believed in and supported this project. Sincere thanks go to her and to the Lila Wallace–Reader's Digest Fund.

Many thanks are due to the poets who have shared their time and talent leading the workshops. Dave Johnson, Clara Sala, Helen Decker, and Melanie Hope know the power of poetry and what it can mean to young adults, whether they read and write poetry for enjoyment or aspire to make it their life's work. These poets combine a love of poetry and a genuine interest in young adults—an unbeatable combination.

A number of young adult librarians have contributed to the success of promoting young adults' awareness of poetry. Caroline Bartels, Patricia Burn, and Jessica Rosokoff were the first three young adult librarians who began this project. Thanks also to Stacy Dillon and Theresa Myrhol at New Dorp Regional Library; Karen Gelover, Veronica Reyes, and Anne Rouyer at 96th Street Regional Library; Sean Flynn at Riverside Branch Library; and Michele Thompson at Allerton Branch Library. These hardworking librarians, who have been the link with local teens, discovered the fun of doing poetry with them and handled the myriad details that make the workshops run smoothly. Without them the poetry workshops and this book would not have happened. Thanks also to the staffs of these libraries who support the work of these young adult librarians. Some of the poems were written in workshops that are not a formal part of Poetry-in-the-Branches. Sincere thanks to the Lee Yaffe Friedman Leventon Fund for supporting the April 1998 poetry workshop at the Jefferson Market Regional Library. Thanks also to Jeff Katz, young adult librarian at the Chatham Square Regional Library, for poems from the spring 1998 Young Adult Poetry Reading held at Chatham Square Library.

Genuine thanks are also extended to Sandra Payne, assistant coordinator of Young Adult Services; Beryl Eber, Manhattan Borough supervising young adult specialist; and Karlan Sick, Bronx Borough supervising young adult specialist. They have provided support in countless ways for poetry work-shops and programs and to the staff who give them. Such expertise and backup is invaluable.

A special acknowledgment and thanks are due to those who have worked on this poetry collection from its earliest stages: Marilee Foglesong, former coordinator of Young Adult Services, and Kay Cassell, associate director of Branch Programs and Services, who, with Lee Briccetti, established the Poetry-in-the-Branches project. Thanks to Karen Van Westering, manager of publications at the Library, for her knowledge and "can do" spirit; and to Ana Cerro of Orchard Books for her enthusiastic support of this book at every stage.

Mary Jane Tacchi, coordinator
Young Adult Services
The New York Public Library

Foreword

Movin' brings together a wide range of young poetic voices from New York City and around the nation. My part in this process was leading poetry workshops along with other talented teaching artists in Poetry-in-the-Branches, a project jointly sponsored by Poets House and The New York Public Library, and then selecting the poems for this anthology. Each teen poet's experience in this program was unique, just as each branch library where the workshops took place reflected the distinct character of the neighborhood surrounding it. Some of these young writers came to the workshops looking to write and share their poetry; some came with reams of poems in hand; and some with just a hope of giving voice to an idea—to create a *move* or to move something or someone, if you will. Others were roaming through the library doing homework and happened upon the workshops. And yet others dropped what they were doing and simply came inside to see what was going down. One young woman, whom I remember in particular, was dancing outside the library with friends while listening to a radio. She was linked to a sizable dog that wore a spiked collar. When the young adult librarian went outside to announce the poetry workshop, the young woman tied her dog to a post near a window so she could keep an eye on it from inside and eagerly rounded up all of her friends to come read and write poems.

In sessions like this, we gathered around a table and read the work of recognized as well as less well-known poets from many different poetic traditions throughout the world. We discussed the poems, and then we wrote our own. The workshops usually ran ninety minutes, but on several occasions, these young writers stayed an extra hour or more, reading, writing, and sharing their work until the library closed for the day.

After each set of workshops, we published a short, usually spiral-bound anthology of the new work and held a publication celebration at the library. Many young poets brought friends and relatives to these parties to hear readings of their original work. These publications were then catalogued and placed in the stacks for other library users to read. It was always exciting to come into the library and hear a young writer tell an older person to check out the anthology in which his or her poems appeared. Writers of every age need publication to make them "legitimate," not only to themselves but often to the authority figures in their lives. One young contributor to *Movin'* recently wrote to me, "Dave, you don't know what this opportunity to publish my poem means to me. My family and friends have never supported my desire to write or read poetry, or even study anything at all. They think I need to be locked up for keeping a journal. Maybe this publication will change their minds. I have learned so much in Poetry-in-the-Branches. Even without being published I know my work has greatly improved, and I am in the practice of writing every day, something I never did before. But to be honest, publishing is exciting. I can't wait!"

For a younger artist, finding communal support is one of the many profound benefits that come from participating in a library workshop. In our groups, we recognize the value of having a place to come together and bandy about all of these possibilities. The ideas that make up our poems are often rooted in our everyday lives, and writing, reading, and sharing help us to become more aware of them. Although consisting of many different voices, the work itself—experimenting with musicality, sound, image, and revision—gives us ground in which to nourish a communal awareness. This work is what makes these poems. Many people think that writing a poem requires a magic elixir. I don't mean that poetry isn't magical—it is. But, ultimately, it is beautifully hard work. Through these endeavors, we hope to create a heightened poetic reality. If so, we can begin to address these ideas metaphorically. And if we are diligent writers, as some of these young adults are, we might even gain the power to resolve conflicts and make significant shifts in our realities. This is hard to do. For many writers it takes a lifetime. But these young writers are getting an early start, and many of them are making the most of it.

Listen to what these young poets have to say. They are not just the "voices of the future." They are also the voices of *now*. Young people have valuable insights to share and should be heard. I know that I learn from them while I'm also teaching them. They are thinkers who, when given an opportunity, contribute richly to our collective dialogue. My hope is that *Movin'* will inspire young writers and the communities in which they live to launch their own poetry workshops and readings and make their own publications happen.

Give these poems a shake, a listen. *Movin'* is hard, fast, sultry, sweet, soft, musical, and flat-out fun! We trust you will delight in reading our moves as much as we did in making them.

Dave Johnson

Movin'

Chopsticks

Hold the chopsticks gently
between your fingers. They should lie
weightless upon your hand, and your
knuckles should be flat. Not
protruding. Your thumb, yes, your
thumb should almost be a straight
line. And the rest of your fingers . . . Watch!
Like this: the first joints peeking like
timid hills, the second joints standing
like calm mountains. Then
let the tips (just the tips) dip
into the bowl, swiftly
but not abruptly. Pick up
a grain of rice. It should rest
delicately between the two sticks.
Bring the chopsticks toward you, not
your face toward the chopsticks.
That grain of rice should become
the tip of your tongue.
Now, swallow.

—*Eva Lou*

Long Lost Friend

On the first day of fourth grade,
you had long hair pulled back, a ponytail.
We only had Enrichment together
and I didn't even know your last name.

In fifth grade—
that's when I took you to the circus,
and I peed in my pants!

In sixth grade there was that boy
who pulled us apart like a strawberry
flying around in a blender.
The day you told me you didn't want
to be friends anymore,
I went home and cried for hours thinking
you had to be lying.

Now I see you on the first day of seventh grade.
You have braces and your hair is cut short.

I'll always know you with long hair.
I'll always know the smell of the banana snowcone
we got all over my Grandma's car on the way
home from the circus.

And even though that boy moved away
and we know he wasn't worth it—
the pain will always be in our hearts.

I just have one question for you.
I haven't been able to figure out—
Where did you go and when are you coming back?

You see, the circus is back in town
and I really want to go.
It's just that my new best friend
really isn't into
that sort of thing.

—*Laura Bierstedt*

If I Could Give Back

(after Stanley Plumly)

If I could give back,

    I would give you the joy of watching

        us sleep.

    I would give you back my life,

    because you almost lost yours for mine.

If I could give back,

I would give you the happy time when

you'd feed me,

the times you taught me how to speak

the little words:

I love you and

Mommy.

           —Stanley Medina

Ice-skating Dreams

Star of the ice
in the Olympic competition,
my woolen skates
slide with ease
over the Vaseline ice
of my old hallway.
Flowers fall from the stands
of stuffed animal friends
but one angry judge
has disapproval in her eyes—

My mother with the mop in her hand—
I wish she was still on the phone.

—Patricia Savage

I wish I didn't feel so old

I used to go camping
with my brother
in the bedroom we once shared.

Sheets draped from bunkbeds,
the green carpet was grass
in the dark,
we would hide from animals
and look at stars
that seemed like they were really there.

We somehow always forgot that
the sky was ceiling,
the animals were shadows,
and we were in a white bedroom
with the door half closed.

—*Chelsea Bunn*

Ode to Eyebrows

Odes are things you do in school.
You never know what to pick.
Eyebrows are things that
rise in confusion, exclaim intrigue.
Conjoined to your forehead, the hairs are fine,
containing genetic information.
Follicles are torn by fingernails
clawing oil in distress.
Eyebrows were not meant to have
their shades named by Revlon on a pencil.
They regulate themselves,
their order, as I cannot do for myself.
Arcs are fine for rockets and doorways:
if only the strands on my head were so smooth.

—*Roberta Winters*

Through the Eyes of a Native American

I hate it when they come and stare.
They buy feathered headdresses and
say "how," trying to imitate us.
They don't know that "how" isn't even our language.
They ooh and ah at our tepee, look at our traditional clothes.
Don't they realize we only keep these for the tourists?
They don't see we have computers and TVs,
just like they do.
Everyone comes and smiles at us.
They're proud they gave us this reservation.
They killed 90 percent of my people and
forced the rest to live here.
They're proud they have "civilized" us "savages."

Sometimes I wish
I could go back to my real home,
to the time the first foreigners came.
I'd kick them out
and keep them out.
We would have no need
to hide ourselves in reservations.
And the only eyes that would stare at me
would look like my own.

—*Mona Xu*

Leaving

I had to leave everything—
the empty swing set of childhood,
swaying in the breeze,
the little room of pink memories,
faded.

Where once it was full of kid
illusions, it now stands, an
empty rectangle,
the window to my fantasies
closed tight, shutting out
the wind that fueled
my dreams.

I'm leaving,
moving to a bigger room,
a bigger place to store
my memories,
my illusions.
It will eventually fill up and then,
I'll move again.

—*Anny Vanegas*

A boy on a tricycle

A boy on a
Red
Tricycle
Hair ablaze
In the sun
Blue
Green
Yellow shirt
Rumbling toward
Marble stairs
The wheels ringing
Like circus music
Eyes focused
Shoulders hunched forward
Concentrating
On the path
Before him
Suddenly
His arms
Turn the handlebars
The other way

—Havila Unrein

Action

I won't stop.

As I sit in the cold metal chair
of my jail cell
I write about the summer—
my men, my friends, my family,
lying next to the
chlorine-filled pool
and writing.

Even when my lethargic body
wants a nap
I write.
When and if I write
doesn't matter
as long as I write.

And when I'm free
I won't stop writing.
I really don't know
what I'm in for.

—*Bethany D. Vivo*

Shoes

They're my old men in rocking chairs,
spitting biographies into the sky.
They're gatherers of stories,
picking up the spit of kings,
the seats of beggars,
and the smell of babies
from crannies in sidewalks
that glitter like a prostitute's makeup
when the sun hits right.

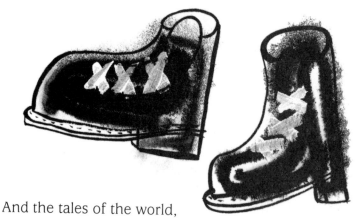

And the tales of the world,
in elegant calligraphy,
are written on their soles.

—*Ben Zeitlin*

Comfort

He sat down on the chair,
running his hands through his hair.
He waited and waited
for five hours straight.
Finally, I sat down next to him.
I asked him gently if he knew.
With his eyes on the floor, he answered, "No."

I told him that she liked the feel of hot sand,
falling from her soft hand.
He told me that she enjoyed the smell of roses
and going on daring adventures.
After a pause, he said, "I love her."
I told him that she'll be fine.
He responded with a slow nod.
Then silence.

After a while, the doctor returned with news of her recovery.
And of the miscarriage.

—*Evelyn Chong*

Movin'

One of these days, I'm outta here.

We moved once,
from Essex to East Houston.
The apartment was nice 'n smooth, seemed
more solid and geometrical
compared to the old compact,
dimly lit space we used to dwell in.
But enough of that.
That move was
insignificant.

One of these days,
I'm flying outta here
on my own
using some high-tech,

    self-sustaining,

        ion-driven,

           compact

              gyroscopic thingy.

Far-fetched,
but who knows what the brilliant
minds of tomorrow will conjure up.

Like,
step into an apparently void space
and you're on Saturn.
Nah . . .
Oh yeah,
me . . .
flying . . .

Where to?
Somewhere
more inviting. . . .

—*Stuart Avineu*

Nothing Could Be Better

I am saddened to realize
I am in math,

on a rainy bad-luck Friday
with a drip faucet nose and no umbrella.

I don't want to be here.
I want to be eating falafel
wrapped in waxed paper
and foil to go.
And mushroom barley soup
served to me by
the waitress
with incredibly long tresses
across from Poets House.

That's all I really want in life—
Falafel and mushroom barley soup,
to be consumed in my own quiet place.

Nowhere near the shadow of math.

—*Toni Ann Fischetti*

I wear many blues

I am blue
Not just one blue . . .
Many blues
The skin I wear is the sea
The nose I wear is royal blue
The hair I wear is light blue
The mouth I have is dark blue
The ears I wear are bird blue
So short am I
Short and blue
A big fat blueberry is what I am
Roly and poly
I am the only blue one
Alone
Scared
With no one to talk to
People would eat me if only they could
Everyone stares at my bluish hair
And the big blue shoes I wear
I know I'm quite different but
That's on the outside
And not on the in
I feel like a parrot among a bunch of pigeons
The fashions will change
But not me, no not me
I am blue

—*Cara Rabin*

ode to the last 5 minutes of english

(for poet Kurtis Lamkin)

deep voice
plucking on the
kora, the 21
strings vibrating like
one month ago or
two when we
decided that you
got the cool award,
the cd,
the heated discussion like africa
like your broadness
against the weather that
made lynn regret
her sandals, her
green veins small

and ms. gannon sat
upfront,
calling back over the
gray plastic chairs
that hurt, all the names
of people we should see,
the largeness
of the tent, the texture
of the grass, the decisions
we could make
with open brackets

—*Shari Goldman Gottlieb*

Change

Growing, emptying and adjusting
my body to the newness;
it's the most unavoidable pain,
this leaving of things, this ending.
I am always moving forward
flowing, following,
moving my feet.
The sadness is like lonely wrists that
shift, borrow, are wide open to pain.
With your eyes you search me.
Those overbearing eyes move forward;
they have questions to be answered
but they, like animals,
ask nothing.

—Caroline Hagood

Place

I'm in a place
where pink is the sky.
I'm green and brown,
grayish hair.

Water is black.
Plants are gray.
The moon is red.
The sun is standing next to the moon,
shining with bright blue.

I'm alone in this place that
I like to call home.
Dragons are nesting up on clouds.
Birds are wingless.
So am I.

So picture me green as I am.
Yes, I am dreaming.
But I fell from a flying horse,
and so did they—

my wings.

—*Epifania Kheilaj Alvarado Vazquetelles*

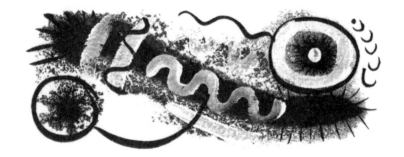

Música

Música es: los sonidos en lazar
el sentimiento expresar y con la voz
entonar una canción sin parar.

Música es: la expresión sublimizada
que se oculta en la cascada en el
canto de las aves cuando vuelan en bandada.

Música es: el susurro de los vientos el
oleaje de las olas el suspirar de los tiempos
y el escuchar de los lamentos.

Música es: el sonar de los clarines el timbrar
de los violines el cantar de serafines de musas
y de querubines.

—*Moisés Reyes*

Music

Translated by Gabriela Kohen

Music is: catching sounds,
expressing feelings,
and setting the tune
to a never-ending song.

Music is: sublime expression
hiding amidst waterfalls
and birdsong,
flying with the flock.

Music is: the whispering of wind,
the crash of a wave,
the sigh of time,
and the telling of tales.

Music is: the blare of a trumpet,
the stroke of a violin,
the singing of angels, muses, and cherubs.

—*Moisés Reyes*

Are We

Are we the dreams of a dreamer
or are we the dreamer that dreams?
Are our lives so complicated
or are they simpler than they seem?
A desk,
      a pencil,
a book, and
      our plight:
We all recognize the black and the white,
and we all know about the dark and the
      light,
but what about what's in between?

—*John Taglialatela*

The Man Hands I Wear

The man hands I wear are shy because
they hide behind my back.
They're big and out of proportion;
they don't feel like my own.

As I walk, my hands pull me forward
and people stare.
They become shy again
and hide behind my back.

Later, they come out again
and I spin around,
the weight of my hands pulling me
this way and that.
Those evil hands,
so big and ugly.

I sit on the stoop of my brownstone,
stuffing those big hands under my thighs,
rocking on them.
I take them out to cover
my wet, teary face and suddenly

they're the best.
They're perfect.
I pat down my fluffy hair
and feel the air rush past
my perfect fingers.
I hold them out for all to see.

See, see.
Hold, hold these perfect hands
and tell me they're not the best,
the softest, and
my own.

—*Lia-taré Brown*

Jealousy

Two girls fighting over a man who can't choose
But neither wants to leave without a fight
Two girls who haven't got a thing to lose
Two girls fighting over a man who can't choose
Two girls who sit and sing the blues
Two girls fighting over a man who can't choose
But neither wants to leave without a fight

—Jasmine Nesbit

Simplicity

If home is where love is,
And love is where trust is,
I guess I'm homeless.

—Nadeema Arshad

Roller skates: the fourthgradeolympicmedalist kind

Skating used to be my passion
>early in the morning
>late at night
>all around my concrete rink

Sewer caps were an excuse
>for tricks
>for spins
>for detours from my regular path

When I fell down
>my crowd helped me up
>or fell down with me

My trainer was never satisfied
>though sometimes
>the raw grace of my wheels
>made her cry

It was skating, my love
    dancing
    for speed
    for strength
    for fun

Up and down
    my narrow black rink
    always the best
    trying to be better

And when I was done
    I would sit and stare
    at my open laces
    thinking up my next routine

—Danielle Sessa

I Once Caught the Ball

It was the girl's varsity volleyball championship game
I was excited
that we made it this far
scared
that we could blow it so easily
and happy
that nothing could be my fault (cause I would NEVER play!!)
yet . . . sad, that it would be over so soon

We lost the 1st of 3 games—
the girl's volleyball championship
Everyone was discouraged
Yet we went on

We won the 2nd game
A long hard game
And we gained back our confidence

Then "why?" I ask
Why did there have to be an injury?
Our star player twisted her knee
Now we knew we'd lost it—

Lost our confidence
     Our strength
         The game
             The CHAMPIONSHIP!

I thought this would be as bad as it could get
Then it got worse—
Of all the girls on the team
He picks me
     Me!!
            Why ME??
So I'm on the court
Aware of all that I can be aware of
Eyeing the ball
From our side
     To their side
         To our side
            To their side
     And back to our side again

8 to 14, them
One more point and we're history
I see the ball comin' straight at me
I go to bump it over the net
And it happened

I CAUGHT THE BALL!!

—*Sona Ahuja*

At the Sidewalk Café, Wednesday Evening, 10:00 P.M.

Launching into notes
her guitar ripping
as if her fingers were teeth
my friend is ten times life size
and speaking in tongues.
Sizzling like hot grease her music spits and
hits its mark.

I imagine everyone is stopped,
paused at their wobbly tables
looking up at her and amazed . . .
But they're not and I'd like to shut them all up:
extinguish their cigarettes,
make the tall guy in front of me scrunch down,
if only I could breathe through the smoke
and see past the spotlight, exploding in the dark.

—*Amy Peltz*

Cartoon

Why am I suddenly a cartoon,
with dark black outlines and
round purple eyes
that I can't blink?

No one takes a child seriously,
much less a cartoon
on a plain white background.

Why don't I have a shadow anymore?
I'm standing on a line
inside a television set in someone's house.

They're watching me like
I'm supposed to do
something.
I can't do it,
so they shut me off.

How can't they care?
They go back to their Monday Night Football
and I have to stand in the dark
until a little boy wants to quit
watching Barney.

And see a different freakish creature.

—Kimberly Chalmers

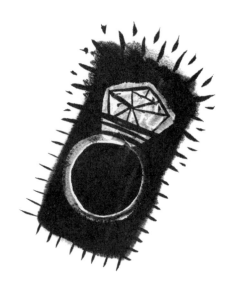

InLine

Bleached blonde hairdo stands in

Lexus lease line and absently

fondles cubic zirconium

wedding ring while imploring adopted

Nicaraguan children to please hush

up and behave properly, like mommy does.

—*Amy Biegelsen*

Day . . . Deli . . . Day

I unlock the cold locks and lift the loud, fast moving gates into my home for the next nine hours. What a long day I am looking into, like a child staring through a pipe to see what's at the other end.

I turn on the lights, saying, *How did I wind up here? Why didn't I do more?* Sure I have my brother who owns the store. He's good to me. And the high school student with the handlebar mustache, he buys a bagel and coffee every morning—he's nice. And that girl—*what's her name?*—with the long, thin legs and beautiful hair. I wish she'd see more than a guy who lets her have breakfast for free.

It's late in the day now. I'm bored. I've mopped and counted the money several times—nothing sold but some cigarettes and donuts. Oh, and one gallon of milk.

That's okay, it'll get busy in an hour, and if it doesn't, then what? I'll work like people who work for my brother—*Wait that's me.* I'm working for my brother, and he's working for the people getting off the train or bus. And they're working for some guy in Manhattan or something. We're all the same.

Everyone, gone now. Time to close up and go home. It's good. I'll feed the neighborhood cats some extra tuna we got in and then watch some Seinfeld and go to sleep. Until the beginning of the next day.

—*Eric Diez*

Alter Ego

(a villanelle)

Lost in confusion and your lies
Vulnerable and naïve is how you view me
I welcome loneliness and face the skies

Unable to feel warmth in your eyes
Through ignorance you still cannot see
Lost in confusion and your lies

I despise the stupidity in your replies
I only smile and let it be
I welcome loneliness and face the skies

I am tuned out to helplessness and ailing cries
See nothing but your deformity
Lost in confusion and your lies

As rapidly as a picked orchid dies
Your deceptions sink in obliquely
I welcome loneliness and face the skies

Becoming Hades' prize
You're dizzy in your uncertainty
Lost in confusion and your lies
I welcome loneliness and face the skies

—Connie Leung

Still Life with Hair Band

to the mathematician folded
collapsed infinity, twisted, folded
it holds—flexible
witness of battle
against the second skin—
wearing away—water torture
a shield
combat fatigue
"snap"
fall out of place
lines, lines
bar code is all that's seen

—*Seung-Min Lee*

haircuts

a
bulb,
centerswing from ceiling, blinks
to yellow a square room,
newspapers
sleep at the floor
and my balloon-bare feet
shift, shift, over, on

I place
a scarfbundle
into open mouth sink
to peel free scissors
with bent waist, plum handles

drymilk tiles exhale frost smoke,
the dancing bulb hums,
pebbles are swept away,
and slender fog follows.
The boulder, now defined.
Callous, it bellows a deep
stomach motion bass
—the Boom shoots dread
through each strand,
burning curling ends—
> a hunt for scissors,
> fingers burst ripe sockets,
> hair cords seized
> the sickle race
> tumble, leap, cut and clear, cut and clear
> every knot, every cluster of
jungle drops
in
muffles.

I shiver,
and bob
to the side,
standing in a wreath of
broken branches, black leaves,
my wrists bow
and the silent storm
swims in my head.

—Suhui Won

If Peaches Had Arms

If peaches had arms,*
one might cut a hole in its side
to relieve the burden
of sweetness
it had been so used to
carrying around.
The juice would flow freely,
but cautiously, at first.
It would drip down the
corner of the table,
along the wooden legs,
and into the sun-soaked fur
of an afternoon cat
that runs against the screeching traffic
of hectic streets and
slides through the door crack of an
inviting little café,
where a girl with a book looks up,
takes a breath, and smells
the sweet heaviness
of burden.

—*Eva Lou*

*First line from Sandra Cisneros, "Peaches—Six in a Tin Bowl, Sarajevo," in My Wicked Wicked Ways (1993)

pisces in the fall

I watch you walk from the bed to the door,
your falling eyelashes taking over
your features, the floor covered in pupils
as you look down, reaching for the knob.

You blur as the door closes behind you.
The glass-filtered sun turns the floor violet
and azure like your cancerous eyes on
skin, my skin burnt from days of pretending

your gaze was a star. I find every crack
in the window and flaw in your strange smile,
stepping in stardust because you look down
too much. Even when you are behind doors

your eyelashes extend out over your
body and blur your features into azure.

—*Dayna Crozier*

Pomegranate

Faceted crimson
gemstones
packaged tightly inside
foamlike layers
organized
perfectly.
Tough leather skin
on the outside
protecting
the valuables
inside.

The time taken
to coax out each seed
only lends pleasure
to the end reward.
Through fighting off
snatching hands
along the way;
the result—a bowl
filled to the brim
with stones
more beautiful than rubies.

A hand carries
the treasure
to the open mouth
waiting
to close and
crush the seeds
like wine grapes
and let the juice
trickle
freely down the throat.

Surely this is
the food of the gods.

—*Kellyn Bardeen*

Resurrection

Last weekend
I walked in on
death at my Uncle Dom's wake.
I sat and cried a little,
fiddled my fingers a lot.
Why do they call it a wake
if the person is dead?
Why can't we wake in this life?

—*Katherine Mango*

About Poets House and The New York Public Library

POETS HOUSE is a place for poetry—a 35,000-volume poetry library and literary center that invites poets and the public to step into the living tradition of poetry. Poets House programs and resources document the range and diversity of modern poetry and stimulate dialogue on issues of poetry in culture.

Poetry-in-the-Branches is a Poets House initiative designed to help community libraries become centers for the discovery of poetry. Launched as a cooperative effort with The New York Public Library in 1994, the program now brings poetry to life in nine branches of The New York Public Library and the Brooklyn Public Library. Poetry-in-the-Branches is an integrated and multilayered approach to developing poetry audiences; it combines readings, writing workshops and discussions for adults and young adults, and poetry displays and collection development with training for librarians.

The poetry included in this book was created in these poetry-writing workshops and also was submitted to *Wordsmiths*, a part of TeenLink, The New York Public

Library's young adult area on its web site. Through *Wordsmiths,* young adults attending Library programs or from points far beyond can submit their prose and poetry for display on-line. TeenLink *(www.nypl.org/branch/teen)* also offers book lists on special topics, links to homework help, fun and games, sports, home pages by teens, and hot lines of interest to teenagers.

THE NEW YORK PUBLIC LIBRARY consists of four major research libraries and eighty-five branch libraries located throughout the Bronx, Manhattan, and Staten Island. The branch libraries form one of the largest urban public library systems in the world. Each year, more than 11 million books, films, recorded materials, magazines, and pictures circulate among the Library's 2.3 million cardholders. These branches reach far beyond the traditional lending role usually associated with neighborhood libraries by providing a wide range of vital services and programs to the community at no charge—among them, Poetry-in-the-Branches.

For more information about Poetry-in-the-Branches, contact Poets House at 72 Spring Street, New York, NY 10012, 212-431-7920; or visit its web site at *http://www.poetshouse.org.*